Randomness

Apurwa Mittal

BookLeaf
Publishing

India | USA | UK

Presentation by *BookLeaf Publishing*

Web: www.bookleafpub.com

E-mail: info@bookleafpub.com

ISBN: 9789363314146

First edition 2024

Dedication

These poems are dedicated to the world around us—the canvas upon which our lives unfold, filled with endless wonders, challenges, and moments of grace. May these verses be a celebration of the richness and diversity of our shared human experience, and a tribute to the profound beauty that surrounds us every day.

ACKNOWLEDGEMENT

Creating this collection of poems has been an incredibly fulfilling journey, and it wouldn't have been possible without the support and encouragement of my family.

First and foremost, I want to thank my Nanu Late Shri Dinesh Raghuvanshi ji , the splendid source of knowledge , who ignited in me the idea of writing .Also, I would thank my parents for their unwavering love and support,specially my mom for encouraging me to write a poetry book To my twin sister Aarya, thank you for always being there for me and for your constant encouragement. Your perspectives have enriched my work in countless ways.

With gratitude,
Apurwa Mittal

PREFACE

Welcome to a collection of poems born from the curiosity and imagination of a teenage poet. Each piece explores a diverse array of topics, chosen at random yet infused with a fresh and candid perspective.

Writing these poems has been a journey of discovery. I've aimed to capture both fleeting moments and profound questions, expressing emotions that are often difficult to articulate. Each poem reflects my wonder at the world—a place both ordinary and extraordinary.

This book invites you to slow down, reflect, and embrace life's randomness. Whether you're a teenager on your own journey or an adult reconnecting with youthful wonder, I hope these poems resonate with you and inspire a renewed sense of curiosity.

Thank you for joining me on this poetic exploration.
With wonder and reflection,

Apurwa Mittal

DREAMSCAPES

What is a dream, and why does it gleam?
Why do they come, in the night's silent stream?
Some bring us hope, some bring us a fright,
One night we soar, the next we fight.

Why do dreams dance in confusion's sway?
Are they just whispers of our day's array?

If dreams reflect our minds' bright flair,
Then let's tread gently, and handle with care.
If we fill our thoughts with joy and light,
Perhaps our dreams will paint the night

.

ECHOES OF BHARAT

India, oh India, a nation not just seen,
But felt in the hearts of millions, vibrant and
serene.
A tapestry of colors, where joy has its own
sound,
A land of countless festivals, where blessings do
abound.

A symphony of faiths, a chorus of belief,
Where many religions merge, giving comfort,
giving relief.
Here, unity takes root, as cultures intertwine,
We grow, we celebrate, like vintage, aging wine.

India, oh India, you're more than just a land,
You're the pulse of a people, forever hand in
hand.
An emotion that binds us, a spirit bold and true,
A journey that we share, a story ever new.
And now you know what India is to me

REDEFINING BEAUTY

Is beauty what we see or what we feel?
Is it blonde hair, flawless skin,
Or the daily mirror's whispered appeal?
Is it the question, "How do I look today?"
Or is it deeper, beyond mere display?

Beauty isn't just a painted face
Or a perfect smile in a crowded place.
It's the heart that feels, the mind that thinks,
The soul that lifts us when it sinks.
It's the way we treat those who fall,
How we lift others, standing tall.

Society paints its flawed design,
Defining beauty with a narrow line.
Why do we value a handsome face
Over the heart's enduring grace?
Why is the surface all we see,
Ignoring depth and empathy?

Admire the person, not just the look.
Find beauty in a thoughtful book.
See the kindness in gentle eyes,
The spark of wisdom, the love that ties.
Cherish the heart that understands,
The tender touch, the helping hands.

Let's redefine what beauty means,
Shatter the mirrors and their screens.
See the soul, the inner light,
The beauty that shines in darkest night.
It's time to change our point of view—
To embrace the beauty that's truly true.

FREEDOM

Yearning for freedom, we seek release,
From work, from taunts, from all unease.
But true freedom lies not in mere escape,
But in finding peace in every shape.

Busy on Sundays, though free from the grind,
Lost in screens, family left behind.
Freedom, we claim, yet chained to our pace,
Missing the beauty of each moment's grace.

To be truly free, look within and see,
Release the mind, let the heart roam free.
For in the present, joy's sweet embrace,
True freedom dwells, in every space.

In the silent whispers of the soul's gentle plea,
Lies the essence of freedom, pure and free.
So let us pause, and in reflection find,
The liberation that dwells within the mind.

For in the stillness of each fleeting hour,
Lies the key to unlock freedom's power.
Embrace the now, let worries cease,
And find in each moment, everlasting peace.

MOVING ON

Some say I've moved on, some say I've not,
But the truth is something only I've got.
It's never easy to simply let go,
No matter what others might claim to know.

Some find the strength, and they move on
through,
Yet many can't, no matter what they do.
It's an illusion that keeps you waiting,
Hoping for someone who won't be returning.

Maybe they've moved on, why can't you?
If it were easy, wouldn't you have too?
But letting go is harder than it seems,
A lingering heartache, chasing old dreams.

Are you sure you miss the person, or just the
memories?
Is it them, or the feeling of being at ease?
Is it the places you visit, or the fact they were
there,
Making each moment seem special, beyond
compare?

In the end, moving on takes time and grace,
To find new paths, to fill that space.
It's not about forgetting, but learning to see,
That happiness awaits, and so does peace for
me.

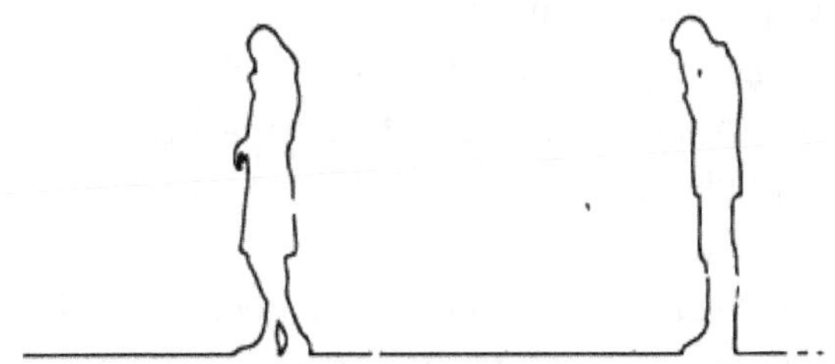

GRATITUDE

In the buzz of city life, where time flies by,
Let's pause, take a moment, and look to the sky.
Amid the chase for more, for things to own,
Let's cherish what we have, make gratitude
known.

In the rush for success, for fame and gold,
Let's savor life's small joys, let happiness unfold.
In this time of wanting, of endless need,
Let's count our blessings, let kindness lead.

Let's thank the universe for this life we hold,
For the love we give, the stories we've told.
But just saying thanks isn't really the deal,
Gratitude runs deeper, it's what we truly feel.

So in the midst of chaos, find a moment to trace,
The beauty in each moment, the joy in each face.
For as humans, with hearts that recall,
Let's dive into gratitude, embracing it all.

GEN-Z

In the world of Gen Z, where tech and life blend,
We're vibing hard and setting trends.
We swipe and scroll with expert hands,
But deep down, we crave something grand.

With memes and jokes, we make our mark,
But real connections light our spark.
In a world of filters and Insta faces,
We're searching for genuine embraces.

We feel the world's struggles, no cap,
Seeking fairness, woke and on tap.
Behind screens, our feels are true,
Hoping for connections that hit different, too.

Navigating situationships and late-night
chit-chats,
Finding meaning in all the snaps.
On socials, we seek something more,
Discovering what life has in store.

Gen Z, a squad finding our way,
Learning from the grind, day by day.
In our quest for depth and more,
We uncover what life has in store.

SEEN IT ALL

From empty promises to shattered trust,
From cherished friendships to faded dust,
I am this way for I've seen it all.

From gentle words to cutting tones,
From joyous laughter to sorrowful groans,
From swift running to a struggling crawl,
I am this way for I've seen it all.

From companionship to standing alone,
From a soft heart turned into stone,
From whispers heeded to ignored calls,
I am this way for I've seen it all.

From radiant smiles to eyes that glare,
From shared laughter to nights of despair,
From bright mornings to rain's lonely fall,
I am this way for I've seen it all.

SOLITUDES'S SILENCE

In whispers, they ask me to share,
Why I hide behind my quiet air,
Do I not like them, or am I blue?
But little do they know, it's not about you.

I'm not an introvert, just a seeker of truth,
My words are not for gossip, but for the beauty
of youth.
If tech and AI fascinate, or space and sky
enthrall,
I'll talk with passion, for hours, without a single
fall.

Living alone is not a prison or a cage,
But a sanctuary, where I can turn the page.
No drama, no noise, no artificial cheer,
Just the stillness of my soul, free from all fear.

In solitude's silence, I find my peace,
A refuge from the world's chaotic release.
I savor each moment, untainted and true,
No distractions, just me, and the beauty that
shines through.

I don't care who leaves or who stays behind,

For in solitude's embrace, I've found my heart
and mind.
I've learned to listen to my inner voice,
And in its wisdom, I've found my soul's choice.

So let me sit alone, with my book and my tea,
And let the world's chaos fade away from me.
For in solitude's silence, I've found my home,
Where love and peace and wisdom are forever
known.

GOALS

In the pursuit of our goals,
How loyal are we?
Do we give our all,
Or do we simply flee?

Hard work and consistency,
Are the keys to success,
If we abandon our goals,
They may become a distant guess.

There are no guarantees,
That we will achieve our aim,
But giving our best effort,
Will leave us with no shame.
If we fall short,
We must rise again,
Failure is but an opportunity,
To learn and gain.

Goals are what drive us,
They keep us awake,
So let's stay loyal,
And give it all it takes.

In the end, we may not win,
But at least we'll have no regret,
For we gave it our all,
And that's the best we can get.

So stay true to your goals,
And keep them in sight,
For with hard work and loyalty,
We can reach the highest height.

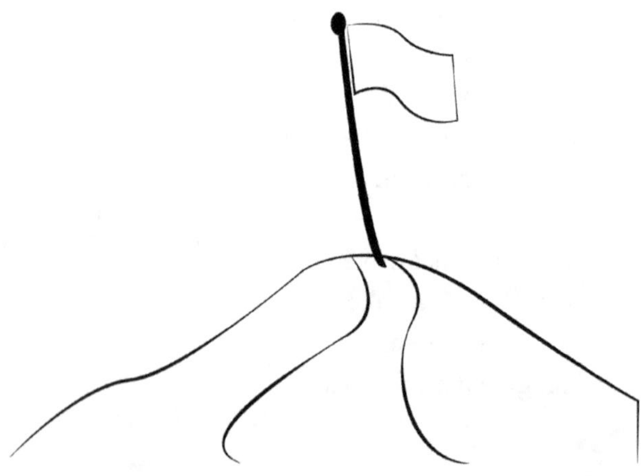

GRANDPARENTS

In the depths of my memory, I recall
Those who first taught me to stand tall,
To walk and talk, to eat and breathe,
Their love and patience, I'll never leave.

But as the years have passed me by,
I find myself asking why
I've grown so distant, so aloof
From the ones who taught me all that's proof

Of their devotion, their sacrifice,
Their endless love, so pure and nice.
Yet somehow I've forgotten it all,
As if their teachings were nothing but small.
Do I not feel ashamed when I declare
That they know nothing, that they're unaware
Of the world and its ways, its twists and turns,
When they were the ones who helped me learn

To navigate through life's stormy seas,
To chase my dreams, to be at ease
With who I am and who I'll become,
All because of them, my shining sun.

They prayed for my success, my joy,
They comforted me when I was a child,

Crying over a scraped knee or broken heart,
Standing with me, never apart.

So let us remember, let us not forget
The ones who gave us all they had to bet
On our futures, our hopes, and dreams,
For in their love, our world gleams.

So cherish them, hold them close,
For they are the ones who matter most.
Don't let time slip away, don't let them go,
For they are the ones who helped us grow.

And when they're gone, let us not be afraid
To say goodbye, to honor their shade,
For in death, as in life, they remain
The ones who taught us to walk in the rain.

TWIN HARMONY: TWO SOULS

In the realm of twins, it's such a delight,
Having someone just like you, both day and
night.
Talking, playing, laughing, we're always in sync,
With a twin by your side, life's just in a blink!

Telepathy's real, we read each other's mind,
A glance, a smile, we're always in kind.
No need for words, we just understand,
In our twin world, it's all so grand.

The closet's doubled, a treasure trove,
Sharing clothes, it's a bond we love.
What's theirs is mine, and mine is theirs,
Twice the style, with plenty to share!

We're opposites, my twin and me,
They're the sun, I'm the shade of a tree.
But together we're balanced, in every way,
Navigating life, come what may.

One thing's for sure, through thick and thin,
Our love for each other, it's a win.
Side by side, through every shine,
Being a twin is just divine!

KARMA

In the realm of karma, where echoes resound,
Actions rebound, in circles profound.
Give of yourself, let kindness be your creed,
In the intricate tapestry of deeds.
Share a cookie, let generosity shine,
For in giving, blessings intertwine.

But tread lightly, for karma keeps score,
No action ignored, no closed door.
Play when you must, but with mindful care,
For karma's return, always there.

In the silent whispers of night's embrace,
Karma's wisdom, a guiding grace.
"Do your best, let go of outcome's sway,"
For in karma's dance, all debts repay.

So journey forth, with karma's light,
In the labyrinth of day and night.
For what you give, returns tenfold,
In the story of karma, truth be told.

"Karma karte jaa, phal ki chinta mat kr."

WEIRDO

In the quiet corners of our soul,
A touch of weirdness takes its toll.
Hidden away, yet shining bright,
A part of us, a guiding light.

Let's embrace the odd, the quirky too,
For in our weirdness, our truth shines through.
In a world of sameness, let's stand tall,
For being ourselves, weird and all.

Tears: A DUAL JOURNEY

Tears, they come, in joy and pain,
A silent language, we can't restrain.
From heartaches deep to triumph's call,
In every tear, emotions sprawl.

Breakups, rejections, they often start,
A torrent of tears, from a broken heart.
But in success, they find their way,
Celebrating victories, come what may.

Yet, in parents' tears, a different hue,
Reflecting love, in all they do.
Whether in pride or sorrow's flight,
Their tears speak volumes, in darkest night.

On every occasion, they find their place,
Weddings, performances, in life's embrace.
But let's not waste them, on futile fears,
Let's save our tears for joyous years.

So may your next tears, in rivers flow,
In moments of triumph, let them glow.
For in every tear, a story unfolds,
Of love, of hope, in hearts enfolded.

THE JOURNEY OF STUDENT LIFE

In the world of books and tests,
In the realm of constant quests,
Lies the charm of student life,
Where wisdom cuts through like a knife.

Days filled with lectures and notes,
Nights spent studying by the light of lamps and
moats,
We strive for grades that sparkle and shine,
To prove our worth, to draw the line.

But beyond the grades and the books,
Lies a journey with many crooks,
For student life is more than just study,
It's about exploring, shaping, living fully.

We struggle, we laugh, we cry,
Through the chaos, we reach for the sky,
For in these defining years of our youth,
We build the pillars of our truth.

It's a time of choices, of paths to take,
Of risks to embrace, of dreams to wake,
For what we sow in these student years,
Will determine our joys, our hopes, our fears.

So let's cherish this time, this precious phase,
Let's learn and grow in countless ways,
For student life, though filled with strife,
Is a gift, a blessing, a chance at life.

So let's raise a toast to student days,
To the lessons learned, the wisdom gained,
For in this journey, we find our voice,
And in our hearts, we forever rejoice.

UNSPOKEN RULES

In a world of silent rules,
Where unspoken norms shape schools,
We walk paths that others tread,
By unseen guides, our lives are led.

From how we dress to how we speak,
These norms, both strong and sometimes weak,
They tell us what is right and wrong,
And guide us as we move along.

Yet norms can change, they're not set in stone,
With courage, we can carve our own.
Let's blend respect with our own voice,
And live our lives by our own choice.

For norms should help, not cage or bind,
Let's free the hearts of all mankind.

CRIES IN THE DARK

Oh, welcome to today's world,
Where everything is bigger, faster, louder,
But the hearts of mankind grow colder,
In this modern age of chaos and disorder.

Girls are told to cover up, to stay at home,
For fear of what may happen if they roam.
But even in the safety of their own abode,
They are not spared from the horror that unfolds.

A 2-year-old, a 60-year-old, it matters not,
In this society where innocence is forgot.
How long must they cry out for help,
Before someone finally hears their desperate
yelp?

We have safer phones, safer homes, safer cars,
But where is the safety in a world so marred
By the atrocities that occur every day,
Yet justice is swift to look the other way.

Five years in jail, it's such a jest,
For lives shattered, hearts distressed.
Injustice reigns, it's plain to see,
In a world where fairness should be.

In every shop, on every street,
Women tremble, their fears discreet.
Blamed and shamed, it's so unjust,
In a world where trust is a must.

Why must she prove her purity,
While he goes free, without scrutiny?
In this double standard, let's make it right,
For a world where justice wins the fight.

NIGHT

Oh, the night, so calm and still,
a time for peace, a time to chill.
Under stars in the sky so high,
we find comfort, and we sigh.

We spend the night with ease and grace,
listening to old songs, finding our place.
Memories of childhood fill our heads,
bedtime stories, snug in our beds.

But remember, night can bring
the darkest fears, the saddest things.
Fear of failing, overthinking's peak,
old sorrows that make us weak.

But just like a coin has two sides,
let's see the good, where love abides.
Thank God for the day just gone,
make peace with everyone before the dawn.

When you wake with morning light,
you'll be glad you spread love in the night.
Be kind, fix what's wrong,
in the night's calm, we all belong.

AND remember its always the darkest before dawn.

ONE SUPREME POWER

Who controls the world? Have you ever
thought?
There is one supreme power who runs it all.
He made us equal, each human the same,
Yet we divide Him, causing sorrow and blame.

We fight and kill to prove our faith is best,
But no God teaches violence or unrest.
Humanity should be our ultimate creed,
All religions teach love, peace, and to heed.

Every faith says to serve and protect,
Whether a dog, a man, a plant, or an insect.
Religion should unite us, not create rifts,
Why do we fight, missing the divine gifts?

It's just one God we've divided in our minds,
Division is fine, but hostility binds.
If you fight, you don't truly worship Him,
For He teaches love, not actions so grim.

What's different about someone of another faith?
They look the same, deserve the same grace.
Treat them with kindness, respect their way,
For we are all human, at the end of the day.

Embrace each belief, see the common thread,
In every prayer, every word said.
Let religion be a bridge, not a wall,
For under one sky, we stand together, all.

LIFE'S ETERNAL CYCLE

Every ending is a new beginning,
A cycle of life, always spinning.
The end of childhood, a cherished phase,
Transitions us into teenage days.

New feelings arise, emotions ignite,
Expectations grow, both day and night.
We learn to study, to party, to chill,
Make friends, lose some, against our will.

Hearts are given, roses too,
Dreams of futures start to brew.
Preparing for careers, we plan our way,
As teenage years begin to sway.

Then comes adulthood, its own fresh start,
Responsibilities now play a part.
The urge to earn, to meet our needs,
To build careers, sow life's seeds.

Setting lifestyles, making our mark,
Adulthood's journey, both bright and dark.
But every end, a new phase unfurls,
As we transition to our later worlds.

Old age arrives, a time to rest,
To thank God for life, we've been blessed.
Reflecting on the path we've led,
Grateful for every step we've tread.

But don't wait until the end to pray,
Thank God throughout, every day.
For in this journey, vast and grand,
We're given life, by divine hand.

So embrace each end, and every start,
With gratitude in your heart.
For every phase, in this life's span,
Is a gift, a part of the master plan.

NIGHTMARE REALITIES

What is your worst nightmare?
Is it the fear of falling off a cliff,
Or the sting of betrayal in the back?
Is it the sorrow of parting ways,
Or the ache of loneliness left behind?
Is it seeing others soar while you wait?

Nightmares aren't just nighttime visions,
But daytime fears we must confront.
Rejection's weight, dreams turned to dust,
Friendships fading, memories undone.

In our darkest times, fears seem real,
Loss and shattered hopes abound.
Yet, nightmares are just passing dreams,
Echoes of fears, not our destiny,
Fading in the light of resilience,
Hope stronger than any fear.

So fear not these fleeting nightmares,
You have the strength to overcome,
To turn fears into new dreams,
And rise above what once held you down.

SPECTRUM OF EMOTION

In the playground of my mind, friends I've
found,
Each with their own laughter, each with their
own frown.
First came Joy, a sprite of endless cheer,
Dancing through moments, devoid of fear.

But as life unfolded, new friends came to stay,
Sadness, solemn and deep, walked a quieter
way.
Alongside, Anger stood tall and stern,
Demanding perfection at every turn.

Then Fear tiptoed in, cautious and wise,
Building walls, wary of surprises.
Midway through life's journey, they held sway,
Guiding steps, keeping danger at bay.

But then, in a rush, puberty's tide,
Brought Anxiety, fretting by my side.
Always worried, about exams or the game,
Interviews looming, casting doubt and shame.

Yet, amidst the turmoil, Love came into view,
A charming face, masking troubles true.
Beneath the surface, a ship's quiet groan,
For love, too, navigates waters unknown.

Before Love arrived, there stood Embarrassment
shy,
Afraid of the limelight, hesitant to try.
Fearful of failure, hesitant to start,
Yet yearning to break free, to play her part.

These are the friends that color my days,
Each one a hue in life's intricate maze.
No one alone can paint the full scene,
For together they mix, a vibrant dream.

For as I embrace them, in laughter and strife,
I learn the beauty of this spectrum of life.

STRENGTH BEHIND TEARS

"People don't cry because they're weak, but
because they've been strong for so long,
Their tears not of surrender, but reflections of
battles they've won.
In the quiet moments, where shadows softly
linger,
Their hearts reveal the depth of their strength, a
silent anchor.

Through trials endured with unwavering grace,
They weathered storms, their spirits finding their
place.
Now, in tears, emotions find release,
A gentle flow marking moments of peace.

So let them weep, these tears so tender and
brave,
For in them, echoes of the courage they've
paved.
Not weakness shown, but a spirit shining
through,
In every drop, a testament to the love they've
held true.

For eyes speak what words cannot, revealing the untold,
Each tear a story, emotions beautifully unfold."